# St. Joseph
## in
# Early
# Christianity

DEVOTION AND THEOLOGY

*A Study and an Anthology of Patristic Texts*

Joseph T. Lienhard, S.J.

SAINT JOSEPH'S UNIVERSITY PRESS

PHILADELPHIA, PENNSYLVANIA

A shorter version of the study preceding the anthology of Patristic texts on St. Joseph was presented as the 8th annual Saint Joseph's Lecture at Saint Joseph's University on March 18, 1999. The annual Saint Joseph's Lecture at Saint Joseph's University was inaugurated in 1992. Its purpose is to explore the rich theological, literary, and artistic tradition that has developed around the person of St. Joseph. It achieves this aim by making accessible to a general audience up-to-date and solid research in this field of scholarly inquiry.

Excerpts from *Origen: Contra Celsum* reprinted with permission of Cambridge University Press; excerpts from the series Fathers of the Church reprinted with permission of The Catholic University of America Press. Acknowledgement is also made to Augsburg Fortress Publishers and to New City Press for permission to use of copyrighted material.

LIBRARY OF CONGRESS CATALOGING-IN-PUBLICATION DATA

Lienhard, Joseph T.
      St. Joseph in early Christianity : devotion & theology : a study and an anthology of patristic texts / Joseph T. Lienhard.
        p.  cm.
      "A shorter version ... was presented as the Saint Joseph's lecture at Saint Joseph's University on March 18, 1999"--T.P. verso.
      Includes bibliographical references
      ISBN 0-916101-29-0
      1. Joseph, Saint. 2. Fathers of the church I Title. II. Title: Saint Joseph in early Christianity.
  BT690.L47 1999
    232.9'32--dc21                            99–29177
                                             CIP

Published by:

**Saint Joseph's University Press**
5600 City Avenue
Philadelphia, Pennsylvania 19131-1395
www.sju.edu/sjupress/

Saint Joseph's University Press is a member of the Association of Jesuit University Presses

# TABLE OF CONTENTS

## STUDY

## ANTHOLOGY

# St. Joseph

## in
## Early
## Christianity

### DEVOTION AND THEOLOGY

## STUDY

# I

# INTRODUCTION

Anyone who speaks about St. Joseph in the early Church should begin with a warning to his hearers: don't expect too much. For the first millennium of Christianity, St. Joseph was all but ignored in preaching, liturgical celebrations, martyrologies, and theological writing. Let me give some examples.

To our knowledge, no Father of the Church ever preached a homily on St. Joseph.

The first known feast of St. Joseph was instituted in Egypt in the seventh century.[1] In all the rest of the Christian Church, there is no feast of St. Joseph before A.D. 1000 at the earliest.[2]

The first treatises on St. Joseph date from the beginning of the fifteenth century, written by Pierre d'Ailly (1350-1420) and Jean Gerson (1363-1429), both theologians at Paris.[3] Isidoro de Isolani, O.P., published a *Summa on the Gifts of St. Joseph*[4] at Pavia in 1522. Thereafter, writings on St. Joseph become frequent.

---

[1] It commemorated Joseph's death, on July 20. The flourishing cult of St. Joseph in Egypt was connected with places that he supposedly visited with Jesus and Mary during their sojourn in Egypt. For several centuries the cult never spread beyond Egypt, perhaps because the Coptic church there was not in communion with other Christian churches. See Francis L. Filas, *Joseph: The Man Closest to Jesus* (Boston: St. Paul Editions, 1962), 479.

[2] Beginning ca. 1000, a feast of St. Joseph gradually spread from the monastery of St. Sabas in Palestine to much of the Eastern church, where Joseph was honored as the last of the Old Testament patriarchs. In the West, St. Joseph first appears in a martyrology, or general calendar of the saints, in the ninth century. A western commemoration of St. Joseph in martyrologies, on March 19, may have begun in Ireland in the ninth century. Such a commemoration was certainly made in the martyrology at Reichenau in the first half of the ninth century. Devotion to St. Joseph then spread to various dioceses and monasteries. A feast of St. Joseph was instituted for Rome in 1479; but only in 1621 was a feast of St. Joseph prescribed for the universal church. Filas, *Joseph: The Man Closest to Jesus*, 482-83.

[3] Pierre d'Ailly, *Tractatus de 12 honoribus S. Joseph*; Jean Gerson, *Considérations sur S. Joseph*.

[4] *Summa de donis S. Ioseph*. The tract is printed, in Latin with a Spanish translation, in Bonifacio Llamera, *Teología de San José*, Biblioteca de autores cristianos, 108 (Madrid: Editorial Católica, 1953).

Perhaps, therefore, this lecture should end here, with the statement: there is no devotion to St. Joseph or theological reflection on him in the early Church.

But it is not quite true to say that. In the early Church—that is, the Church up to the end of the Roman Empire, ca. 600—speculation on Joseph is scattered, but it exists. And what is scattered can be gathered.

Before I begin gathering, however, let me sketch a few characteristics of the early Church: who theologians were, how Scripture was read, what the Church's doctrinal concerns were, and who were honored as saints.

In the early Church, theologians were pastors. They wrote to teach the people and to protect their faith. By contrast, in the early Middle Ages theologians were monks, pondering their own salvation. And from the thirteenth century on, theologians have been university professors, intent on impressing their students and gaining recognition from their colleagues.

Then too, in the early Church, Scripture was read very differently than it is now. In antiquity, secular education for young men consisted in the intense study of a text considered sacred—Homer for Greeks, Vergil for Latin speakers. The study was made word by word, since the basic unit of understanding was not the sentence or the narrative unit but the word.[5] Educated men who converted to Christianity took this method of studying a text with them. The Fathers' sacred book was the Bible, and they spent a great deal of their time reading it, preaching about it, and commenting on it—precisely word by word. St. Augustine's longest work—to give only one example—is not the formidable *City of God* but his *Explanations of the Psalms*. Thus, for example, we need not be amazed when the Fathers spend page after page explaining the divergent genealogies of Jesus in the gospels of Matthew and of Luke.

---

[5] See Joseph T. Lienhard, "Reading the Bible and Learning to Read: The Influence of Education on St. Augustine's Exegesis," *Augustinian Studies* 27 (1995): 7-25.

In their study of the Bible, moreover, the Fathers accepted in faith three controlling truths: **the Holy Spirit is one,** and thus, in the whole Bible, speaks with one voice and teaches one truth; **the Holy Spirit is no fool**, and nothing in the Bible is trivial or irrelevant; and **the Holy Spirit speaks to me**, so that everything the Bible says should, when understood rightly, foster my Christian faith and life. With these principles, the Fathers set out to study and explain the Bible, and we will see these principles illustrated many times.

Further, the early centuries were the time when the Christian Church unfolded its essential doctrines: the doctrines of the Trinity and of the person of Christ. All of Christian theology can be considered to be the answer to one question, the question that Jesus put to his disciples, "And who do you say that I am?" (Mk 8:29). The Christian Church worked out its answer to the Lord's question in the course of several centuries. Jesus the Christ, our Savior, is both divine and human. As divine, he is the second person of the Blessed Trinity, God in the same way that the Father is, but also the Father's Son, Word, Wisdom, Power, and Image. As man, he is man in the same way that we are. As Son of God, he has a Father but no mother; as Son of Man he has a mother but no father. One way to express the hypostatic union of divine and human natures in Christ is to acknowledge Mary, his mother, as *Theotokos*, "God-bearer." Mary, who conceived him as a virgin, remained a virgin throughout her life. Into this sketch of Christian doctrine, not only did Joseph not fit, but in a sense he had to be absent: he was not the human father of Jesus, nor could Mary have borne any other children by him after Jesus' birth. Even to call Joseph Mary's husband seemed vaguely inappropriate.

Finally, in the early Church, saints were martyrs and martyrs were saints, beginning with St. Stephen and St. James and continuing through the thousands (but not hundreds of thousands) who died for the Christian faith under the emperors Decius, Valerian, and Diocletian. The apostles, too, were acknowedged as martyrs, beginning with Peter and Paul in Rome. John the Baptist was a martyr. A few non-martyrs were venerated as saints, but Joseph was not.

What, then, did early Christianity say about Joseph? The answer is, in a way, dialectical. Beginning in the mid-second century, writings called the apocryphal New Testament treated, among many other themes, the childhood of Jesus and of Mary. These writings defended Christ's divinity and Mary's virginity, but at a price: they depicted Joseph as an old man and a widower, and sometimes as a fool. Some of the Fathers accepted legends from the New Testament apocrypha. Others, though, reacted against the apocrypha, approached Joseph through the study of difficult New Testament texts, and, basing their thought on sound doctrine, made more balanced statements about Joseph. We will see many details about Joseph in the Fathers, both eastern and western. If there is one point that divides East and West, it is that the East, following the lead of the apocrypha, generally saw Joseph as Mary's protector, an an elderly widower with adult children from his previous marriage. The West, beginning with Jerome and Augustine, taught that Joseph was a virgin. And Augustine will also be the strongest defender of a true marriage between Mary and Joseph.

We begin now to look at some details. And there will be many details to consider before a clear picture emerges.

# II

## JOSEPH IN THE
## APOCRYPHAL NEW TESTAMENT

Beginning in the early second century, Christian writers—some pious, some creative, some heretical—composed writings in the four literary genres of the New Testament books: gospels, acts, epistles, apocalypses. We know the names of several dozen gospels, half a dozen acts of apostles, various epistles, and some apocalypses. In a few cases we have complete texts of the works; in more cases we have only fragments of the text or quotations gathered from other writings; in still other cases we have no more than a name. These works vary widely in content, style, and orthodoxy, from bland literary exercises like the *Epistle to the Laodicenes* to fully heretical works like the Gnostic gospels.

For the consideration of Joseph, six such works are important:

1. the *Protoevangelium of James*, from the latter half of the second century;[6]
2. the *Gospel of Thomas*, or *Infancy Story of Thomas*, perhaps from the mid-third century;[7]
3. the *Gospel of Pseudo-Matthew*, from the fifth century, a work that conflates and expands the two previous works;[8]
4. the *Nativity of Mary*,[9] an expansion of Pseudo-Matthew;

---

[6] Also called the *Book of James*. English translation in Montague Rhodes James, *The Apocryphal New Testament* (Oxford: Clarendon, 1924), 38-49 and E. Hennecke, *New Testament Apocrypha*, ed. W. Schneemelcher, trans. R. McL. Wilson (London: SCM, 1963), 1:374-88.

[7] English translation in James, *Apocryphal NT*, 49-65 and Hennecke, *NT Apocrypha*, 1: 392-401.

[8] Also called the *Book of the Infancy*. Excerpts in James, *Apocryphal NT*, 70-79 and Hennecke, *NT Apocrypha*, 1: 410-13.

[9] Also called the *Gospel of the Birth of Mary*. See James, *Apocryphal NT*, 79-80.

5. the *Arabic Gospel of the Infancy*,[10] mostly a compilation from other books; and finally,

6. the Coptic *History of Joseph the Carpenter*.[11]

Of these six works, the *Protoevangelium of James* is clearly the earliest and by far the most significant. The work is about Mary, beginning with her miraculous conception and ending with the birth of Jesus. Despite its status as an apocryphon, the *Protoevangelium* influenced the Church's liturgy. In the Roman Calendar now in use, for example, the memorial of Sts. Joachim[12] and Ann, parents of Mary, on July 26, and the memorial of the Presentation of Mary in the Temple, on November 21, both depend on the *Protoevangelium*. For our purposes, the *Protoevangelium* makes some important, if rather problematic, statements about Joseph. Let me paraphrase the narrative briefly.

Joachim and Anna are sterile until an angel tells Anna that she will conceive a child. Mary is born of her parents' union. When she is three years old, Joachim and Anna bring her to live in the temple. She stays there until she is twelve. Then an angel orders the high priest to assemble all the widowers of the people; a miraculous sign will designate the one to care for Mary. The widowers give their staffs to the high priest. After the high priest prays, he gives the staffs back to the widowers. A dove flies out of Joseph's staff and lands on his head.[13] The priest tries to give Mary to Joseph, but Joseph protests: he already has two sons and, because of his age, the relationship with Mary would make him look ridiculous. But after being reassured, Joseph accepts Mary—that is, he "takes her under his care," but is never said to marry

---

10 Excerpts in James, *Apocryphal NT*, 80-82 and Hennecke, *NT Apocrypha*, 1: 408-9.

11 Also called the *Death of Joseph*. See James, *Apocryphal NT*, 84-86.

12 Augustine doubted that the name of Mary's father was Joachim (*Against Faustus the Manichee* 23, 9). St. Pius V (1566-72) suppressed the feast of St. Joachim, but Paul V (1605-21) reintroduced it.

13 Cf. the narrative about the staff of Aaron in Num 17:1-11. The staff is a symbol of Joseph's election. The lily, which first appears in Joseph's hand in early-fourteenth-century art, is a symbol of purity and virginity rather than election.

her; and as soon as he brings Mary into his home he goes away for six months to build buildings.

Later in the narrative the author paraphrases the gospel accounts of Joseph's learning of Mary's pregnancy and desiring to divorce her. The account in the *Protoevangelium* is more dramatic and rhetorical than the gospels are, but not different from them, except that the *Protoevangelium* has Mary and Joseph undergo an ordeal at the hands of the high priest, drinking "the waters of conviction."[14] Both Joseph and Mary are vindicated of any charge of wrongdoing.

In a third scene, in Bethlehem, Mary is in labor. Joseph leaves her in the care of his two sons and seeks a Hebrew midwife. He assures the midwife that Mary is his betrothed, not his wife. As the midwife approaches the cave, Jesus is born, apparently miraculously. In a tasteless detail, a companion of the midwife, named Salome, tries to ascertain that Mary is still a virgin, and her hand falls off. The hand is restored when she touches the infant Jesus.

Thus, in this early work, we see several important, but problematic, assertions that are not accounted for in the gospels:

1. Joseph was far older than Mary, which makes him less tempted to violate her virginity.

2. Joseph was a widower with children, which explains the gospel passages about the brothers and sisters of Jesus.

3. Joseph is reluctant to take Mary, which suggests reverence and awe for her, rather than desire.

4. Joseph is portrayed as the divinely elected companion or protector of Mary, not her husband, which allows the author to avoid writing of their "marriage."

The other New Testament apocrypha merely amplify and exaggerate these details. The bizarre *Gospel of Thomas*, for example, portrays the Child Jesus essentially as a divine brat. He strikes another boy dead for hitting him and then raises him from the dead. The same

---

[14] Cf. Num 5:12.

apocryphon portrays Joseph as incompetent. In his shop he cuts a board too short; Jesus simply pulls on the board and makes it the right length. As in other apocrypha, the stupidity of Joseph is presumed to glorify Christ. The *Gospel of Pseudo-Matthew* expands what the *Protoevangelium* began: Joseph is now a grandfather, and even his grandchildren are older than Mary. Pseudo-Matthew also fends off the idea of a true marriage between Joseph and Mary by having Mary make a vow of perpetual virginity and thus become a Christian nun long before nuns existed. The Coptic *History of Joseph the Carpenter* depicts Joseph as an aged widower with six children and even gives a chronology: Joseph marries at 40, becomes a widower at 89, receives Mary at 91, and dies at 111. The *Arabic Gospel of the Infancy* enlarges on the picture of Joseph as incompetent, whose carpentry was regularly accomplished only by Jesus' miraculous intervention.

The motivation behind the apocrypha may have been right: that is, to defend Christian doctrine, but the solutions they proffered raised far more problems than they solved. Any further interpretation of Joseph, therefore, had to counter some of these misguided traditions from the apocryphal writings.

# III

# JOSEPH IN THE
# WRITINGS OF THE FATHERS

We turn now to the Fathers of the Church, those Christian writers and theologians, some great and some not so great, who wrote from the second century to the seventh. The Fathers were concerned, first of all, with the right interpretation of the Bible, and then with true doctrine. Their statements about Joseph can be summarized under five questions. Two are biblical, two are doctrinal, and one will serve as a conclusion.

The two biblical questions are these:

1. How can Joseph's double genealogy be explained? Was he the son of Jacob, as Matthew records (Mt 1:16) or the son of Heli, as Luke records (Lk 3:23)?

2. How can the references in the gospels to the brothers and sisters of Jesus be explained? And, in light of the answer to this question, was Joseph a widower or a virgin?

Two questions are more doctrinal than exegetical:

3. Did Joseph contract a true marriage with Mary?

4. May Joseph be called the "father" of Jesus?

And finally, there is a devotional question that will lead us to some conclusions:

5. Can we detect, in the writings of the Fathers, the seeds of a cult of Joseph as a Christian saint?

## 1. THE DOUBLE GENEALOGY OF JESUS

The facts about Jesus' genealogy are simple. Matthew's gospel, at the beginning of chapter 1, traces Jesus' descent from Abraham through David to Joseph through forty-two generations and gives the name of Joseph's father as Jacob (Mt 1:1-16). Luke's gospel, in chapter 3—that is, after Jesus' baptism—traces Jesus' ancestry back from Joseph through David and Abraham to Adam, and ultimately to God, through seventy-seven generations (Lk 3:23-38). Luke gives the name of Joseph's father as Heli. Moreover, Matthew and Luke have different series of names for the generations between David and Joseph.

These texts raised two problems for the Fathers of the Church.

The first problem was the truth of the gospels. Pagan critics ridiculed the Christian Scriptures for failing to agree even on Jesus' ancestry. Augustine quotes one critic on just this point: "If I shall find a falsehood [in the Gospel], you certainly will not then believe [the Gospel]; and I have found [one]."[15] And Faustus the Manichee, in a debate with Augustine, said, "I long tried to persuade myself . . . that God was born; but the discrepancy in the genealogies of Luke and Matthew made me stumble, as I knew not which to follow."[16]

The difficulty became more acute by the middle of the second century, when a scurrilous legend spread about the paternity of Jesus. Origen quotes the story from his anti-Christian opponent, Celsus.[17] Some enemies of Christianity said that Jesus was the illegitimate child of Mary and a Roman soldier. The soldier was even given a name, Panthera.[18] The legend had it that Joseph the carpenter discovered Mary's adultery and drove her out of his house, and that Mary concocted the story of the virginal conception to conceal her adultery.

The second problem, for Christians, was the fact that the gospels, while denying that Joseph was Jesus' father, traced Jesus' ancestry through Joseph (Mt 1:16; Lk 3:23).

---

[15] Augustine, Sermon 51, 11.

[16] Augustine, *Against Faustus the Manichee* 3, 1 (trans. Richard Stothert, NPNF 1, 4, 159, altered).

[17] Origen, *Against Celsus* 1, 28; 1, 32 (texts 5 and 6).

[18] The simplest explanation of this unusual name is that it is a corruption of the Greek word *parthenos*, which means "virgin," as if those unfamiliar with Christian teaching heard Christians say that Jesus was the son of Mary and Parthenos, instead of "son of Mary the Virgin."

To the first problem, the Fathers offered several solutions: either Jacob and Heli were half brothers; or Joseph was adopted; or the gospels give two genealogies for Jesus, one royal and one priestly.

The earliest known attempt to explain the double genealogy was made by Julius Africanus (ca. 160-ca. 240), a Christian writer from Palestine and the author of a set of chronological tables. Africanus was interested in the details of Scripture and addressed a letter to Origen questioning the story of Susanna in the Book of Daniel. In a letter addressed to a man named Aristides, probably the man who had posed the problem of the double genealogy to him, Africanus supplied a complicated but intriguing answer.

(A prenote: the gospel genealogies, besides listing two different fathers for Joseph, also list two different grandfathers, Matthan [in Matthew] and Matthat [in Luke]. For reasons we can no longer discern, Africanus calls Joseph's grandfather Melchi, who according to Luke was his great-great-grandfather.)

Africanus bases his solution on the levirate[19] law of Dt 25:5-7, according to which, when a man died childless, his brother was to marry his widow to continue the dead man's line, and the first child the woman bore to him would be reckoned as the dead husband's offspring. Africanus hypothesizes that Matthan, Joseph's grandfather, married a woman named Estha, and she bore him a son, Jacob. Matthan then died, and Estha married again, this time a man named Melchi. By Melchi she also bore a son, Heli. Thus Jacob and Heli were half brothers. Heli married but died childless. Jacob then married Heli's widow, fulfilling the levirate law, and begot Joseph. Joseph was thus the natural son of Jacob but the legal son of Heli, and Joseph's two "fathers" and the divergent ancestry are both explained. Africanus points out, correctly, that Matthew uses the word "beget" in his genealogy, but Luke does not; thus Luke does not specify a biological relationship between Joseph and Heli, any more than he does between Adam and God.

---

[19] From the Latin *levir*, brother-in-law.

Africanus's solution was clever but not without its problems. There is no sure evidence that the levirate law applied to half brothers of the same mother. Yet Africanus's explanation gained widespread acceptance. Eusebius preserved the letter in his great work, the *Ecclesiastical History*, which was translated into Latin early in the fifth century and read throughout the Middle Ages.

For most of his life, Augustine proposed a simpler solution: namely, that Joseph was born into one family and adopted into another after his father died: that is, Matthew names Joseph's natural father and Luke his adoptive father.[20] But some time after 418 he read Africanus's letter and adopts his solution, based on the levirate law.[21]

A third solution, that the two genealogies represent two distinct functions of Christ, was proposed by several Fathers. The first to hint at this solution was Origen, who wrote near the middle of the third century. He was one of the most creative, if sometimes erratic, exegetes of the early Church. Origen points out that Matthew gives Jesus' genealogy before his baptism (always with the word "begot"), while Luke gives it after the baptism by John (always without "begot"). He also notes that Matthew presents Jesus' descent from David through Solomon, whereas Luke presents it through Nathan (whom Origen takes to be the prophet Nathan). But baptism is rebirth, and in baptism, therefore, Jesus receives a new genealogy. His old genealogy, Origen suggests, was royal, through King Solomon; his new one is prophetic, through Nathan.[22]

Eusebius of Caesarea, early in the fourth century, considered a similar solution, which he said was proposed by some Christians, but then rejected it as a "praiseworthy error."[23] These Christians, he writes, hold that the double genealogy, through Solomon and Nathan,

---

[20] Augustine, *On the Harmony of the Gospels* 2, 3, 5 (text 32); Sermon 51, 27-28 (texts 42 and 43); *Against Faustus the Manichee* 33, 2.

[21] Augustine, *Retractations* 33, 2 (text 47).

[22] Origen, *Homilies on Luke* 28, 3 (text 14).

[23] Eusebius of Caesarea, *Quaestiones evangelicae ad Stephanum* 4, 1 (PG 22, 900).

represents Christ's dual functions, as king and as priest. But Eusebius rejects the solution on the grounds that both genealogies in the gospels are Davidic and hence from the tribe of Judah, whereas priests came from the tribe of Levi.

Augustine has the fullest explanation of the double genealogy as signifying Christ's dual function, royal and priestly.[24] Matthew, he writes, traces Jesus' royal line downwards through Solomon. It was with Bathsheba, Solomon's mother, that David sinned; so, as king, Christ came down to take on our sins in his mortal flesh and to show us how to fight and conquer. Matthew places the genealogy at the beginning of his gospel, whereas Luke places it after Jesus' baptism to prefigure our being cleansed from sin. And when Luke traces Jesus' genealogy upwards, he signifies our ascent after the abolition of sin. Luke traces Jesus' ancestry through Nathan, who rebuked David for his sin with Bathsheba.

Augustine then raises the problem that Eusebius saw: both Joseph and Mary were from the house of David and not from the priestly tribe of Levi. From David on, he notes, there are two families: the royal, descending from David, and the priestly, ascending to David. Yet the Lord is not from the priestly tribe of Levi, for the Lord was to put an end to the sacrifices of the temporary, Levitical priesthood and, by the holocaust of himself, become the eternal priest in the order of Melchisedek. Nathan represents this new priesthood. Thus Augustine completes the spiritual interpretation of the double genealogy.

The second problem was: why did the evangelists give Joseph's ancestry and not Mary's? In answer, many Fathers wrote that Joseph and Mary were close relatives, as did, for example, Ambrose and Jerome. Ambrose writes that, since both Joseph and Mary registered for the census in Bethlehem, both must have been from the same tribe and city and thus closely related.[25] Jerome uses the same argument and adds

---

[24] Augustine, *On Eighty-Three Different Questions* 61, 2. See also *On the Harmony of the Gospels* 1, 3, 5.

[25] Ambrose, *Commentary on Luke* 3, 3-4 (text 22).

that it is not the custom of Scripture to include women in genealogies.[26] Augustine quotes Rom 1:3 ("descended from David according to the flesh") to show that Jesus was certainly of Davidic descent. He also argues that, since Joseph had paternal authority over Jesus, Jesus was rightly called his son.[27] In general, though, the problem of Jesus' ancestry being traced through Joseph did not raise serious doctrinal problems for the Fathers, and they treat it cursorily.

The legend of the soldier Panthera attested by Celsus also lived on and took new shapes among the orthodox. Hegisippus, in the second century, had postulated that Joseph had a brother named Clopas. According to Mk 15:40, Mary of Clopas was the father of James and Joseph; thus James and Joseph were Jesus' cousins. Epiphanius of Salamis, the anti-heretical writer of the late fourth century, takes up Hegesippus's statement that Joseph had a brother named Clopas and adds that their father, Jacob, was surnamed Jacob Panther.[28] Thus Panther, in anti-Christian legend the Roman soldier who was Jesus' father through Mary's adultery, becomes Jesus' grandfather. Later still, John of Damascus combined the traditions further and tried "to show that Joseph and Mary were related—through a 'Panther' who was the great-grandfather of Mary via Joachim and the great-granduncle of St. Joseph via Heli."[29]

## 2. THE BROTHERS AND SISTERS OF JESUS; AND, WAS JOSEPH A WIDOWER OR A VIRGIN?

The apocrypha, beginning with the *Protoevangelium*, portrayed Joseph as a widower with children and thus significantly older than Mary. An easy explanation of the brothers (and sisters) of Jesus was

---

[26] Jerome, *Commentary on Matthew* 1, on Mt 1:18 (text 18).

[27] Augustine, Sermon 51, 16 (text 35).

[28] Epiphanius, *Panarion* 78, 7, 5.

[29] Filas, *Joseph: The Man Closest to Jesus*, 48, referring to John of Damascus, *On the Orthodox* Faith 4, 14.

thereby available, and Joseph's respect for Mary's perpetual virginity became more credible. The Coptic *History of Joseph the Carpenter* represents an extreme: Joseph has six children, and grandchildren besides, and receives Mary at the age of 91. In such speculation the indignity of partners who, as the Gospel implies, were to be perceived as married, yet whose age differed by more than 75 years, is ignored. The indignity is supposedly eased by suggesting that Mary and Joseph did not have a true marriage; Joseph was Mary's protector or guardian rather than her husband.

In general, the Eastern church accepted the basic thrust of the apocrypha and assumed that Joseph was a widower with children. The Western church moved in the same direction for a while. But Jerome, in the late fourth century, vigorously insisted that Joseph was a virgin. Augustine followed Jerome on this point, and theologians in the Middle Ages generally followed their lead.

Among the Eastern Fathers, Origen explained that the attribution of children to Joseph by an earlier marriage was a way of safeguarding Mary's virginity; he is one of the few Fathers to mention this doctrinal motive explicitly.[30] He also denied that Joseph was, or could have been, a virgin; Jesus and Mary had to be the "firstfruits" of virginity.[31] Epiphanius of Salamis, at the end of the fourth century, attributed six children to Joseph, all from a previous marriage.[32] Epiphanius was probably the main conduit through which this position flowed into the Eastern church.

In the West, Hilary accepted the position that Joseph had children from a previous marriage.[33] Ambrose writes that in the Scriptures the

---

[30] Origen, *Commentary on Matthew* 10, 17 (text 15).

[31] Ibid.

[32] Epiphanius, *Ancoratus* 60, 1 (Joseph's six children were James the brother of the Lord, Simon, Judas, Joses, Anna, and Salome); *Panarion* 28, 7, 6 (Joseph had four sons); 51, 10, 7-8 (Joseph was 80 years old and had six children when he received Mary); 78, 7, 2-9 (a letter by Epiphanius in which he mentions four sons and two daughters, and also Panther; see above).

[33] Hilary, *Commentary on Matthew* 1, 4 (text 26).

name "brethren" embraced a far wider group than offspring of the same parents. He adds that the brethren of Jesus might have been from Joseph, not Mary, but shows little interest in pursuing the question.[34] Jerome, who held that Joseph was a virgin, insisted vigorously that the brethren of the Lord were not Joseph's children but cousins of Jesus.[35]

With Jerome and Augustine a doctrinal tradition began that took root in the West and persisted there. Jerome, in his work against Helvidius written in 383, argues for Joseph's virginity by association and appropriateness. He is part of the wave of asceticism that gripped the West in the late fourth century; he attributes the ascetical ideal of virginity, long affirmed of Jesus and Mary, to Joseph also. "Joseph himself," Jerome writes, "was a virgin through Mary, so that a virgin son might be born of a virgin wedlock."[36] "He who was deemed worthy to be called the father of the Lord remained a virgin, with Mary."[37]

Augustine's doctrine on Joseph's virginity underwent some stages of development. In a work written before he was ordained a bishop, he speculated that the brethren of Jesus might be Joseph's children,[38] but he never mentions the theory again. On the contrary, five years later, in his treatise *On the Work of Monks*, he clearly affirms that Joseph was perpetually a virgin.[39] Thereafter Augustine continued to defend Joseph's purity, in Sermon 51 and in his first work against Julian. "His greater purity confirms his fatherhood," Augustine writes, "as he was a chaste husband, so he was a chaste father."[40] A little later, Augustine writes against Julian: "When he saw the holy virgin already fruitful with the divine gift, he did not seek another wife, although he would

---

[34] Ambrose, *On the Consecration of a Virgin* 6, 43 (text 24).

[35] Jerome, *Commentary on Matthew* 2, on Mt 12:49-50 (text 19).

[36] Jerome, *Against Helvidius* 19 (text 17).

[37] Ibid.

[38] Augustine, *Exposition of the Epistle to the Galatians* 8, 5 (text 27).

[39] Augustine, *On the Work of Monks* 13, 14 (text 33).

[40] Augustine, Sermon 51, 30.

never have sought the virgin herself if she had not needed a husband. He did not think the bond of conjugal faith should be dissolved because the hope of carnal intercourse had been taken away."[41] Passages like these, and the absence of any further references to Joseph's previous marriage, make it clear that Augustine, for most of his time as bishop, held that Joseph was a virgin.

Western teaching on the virginity of Joseph grows even clearer after Augustine. The virginity of Joseph is vigorously defended in a Pseudo-Augustinian sermon from North Africa in the sixth century[42] and became a common teaching in the Latin Middle Ages.[43]

### 3. Did Joseph Contract a True Marriage?

The Gospel according to Matthew twice calls Mary Joseph's wife[44] and twice calls Joseph Mary's husband.[45] But the apocryphal New Testament, apparently out of doctrinal anxiety, shied away from these terms.

In many ways the whole point turns on the definition of marriage. So long as marriage was understood to be constituted by consummation, as it generally was, the Fathers could not assert that Mary and Joseph had a true marriage. Hilary of Poitiers, for example, in his *Commentary on Matthew*, wrote, "Because she was betrothed, she is received as a wife. She is 'known' as such after her childbirth—that is, she advances to receive the name 'wife.' She is 'known' [as wife], but she has no relations [with Joseph]. …Whenever there is a question of these two [that is, Jesus and Joseph], she is called rather the mother of

---

[41] Augustine, *Against Julian* 5, 12, 48 (text 46).

[42] Ps-Augustine, Sermon 195, 6 (text 49).

[43] So Alcuin, Rabanus Maurus, Peter Damian, Rupert of Deutz, Peter Abelard, Hugh of St. Victor, Peter Lombard, Peter Comestor, Peter of Riga, Albert the Great, and Thomas Aquinas. See texts in Urbanus Holzmeister, *De sancto Ioseph quaestiones biblicae* (Rome: Pontificium Institutum Biblicum, 1945), 65.

[44] Mt 1:20, 24.

[45] Mt 1:16, 19.

Christ [cf. Mt 2:13, 20; Lk 2:33], because that she was, not the wife of Joseph, for that she was not.... Therefore the betrothed also received the name of wife and after the childbirth, having been recognized as wife, she is presented only as the mother of Jesus."[46] Maximus of Turin (the second fifth-century bishop of that name) wrote, "Joseph was always the betrothed, but never the husband."[47] A homily by Pseudo-Origen on Matthew, influential in the West because it was read in the Divine Office until the sixteenth century, also denied that Mary and Joseph had a true marriage. The homilist has the angel say to Joseph, "Even though she is named your wife,... she is not your wife, but rather the chosen mother of the only-begotten God."[48] Closer to Augustine, the Pelagian Julian of Eclanum denied that Joseph and Mary had a true marriage, arguing, "Because there was no intercourse, there was no marriage."[49]

A turn came with Ambrose and Augustine, who defended the marriage of Joseph and Mary as a true marriage. Their ground for this assertion was Roman law. In Roman law marriage was constituted by consent, not by consummation. A classical phrase in Justinian's *Digests* expresses this understanding concisely: the *Digests*, quoting Ulpian, state: "it is not intercourse, but consent, that makes a marriage" ("nuptias non concubitus, sed consensus facit").[50] The opposing view, represented by (among others) Julian of Eclanum, that sexual relations constitute marriage, seems to derive not from a different legal tradition (Julian was at least as much a Roman as Augustine was), but from a popular assumption or attitude.

In passages on the marriage of Joseph and Mary in his *Commentary on Luke* and his work *On the Consecration of a Virgin*, Ambrose employs several terms drawn from Roman law or from the language of jurists.

---

[46] Hilary, *Commentary on Matthew* 1, 3 (text 25).

[47] Maximus of Turin, Sermon 53 (PL 57, 639A). This Maximus was bishop from 451 to 465.

[48] Ps-Origen, *Homily 17: On the Vigil of the Lord's Nativity* (text 50).

[49] Quoted by Augustine in *Against Julian* 5, 12, 46.

[50] *Digesta Iustiniani* 50, 17, 30 (ed. Th. Mommsen [Berlin: Weidmann, 1870], 2: 958).

What constitutes a marriage, Ambrose writes in his *Commentary on Luke*, is not the loss of virginity but the solemn affirming of the marriage (*coniugii testificatio*) and the celebration of the wedding (*nuptiarum celebratio*).[51] In his work *On the Consecration of a Virgin*, he writes that a marriage is constituted by the conjugal contract (*pactio coniugalis*).[52]

Augustine develops at length his teaching that Joseph and Mary contracted a true marriage. He writes in Sermon 51, "Joseph then was not the less his father, because he knew not the mother of our Lord, as though concupiscence and not conjugal love (*caritas coniugalis*) constituted the marriage bond."[53] What makes a woman a wife, he writes, is not lust (libido) but conjugal love. Augustine demonstrates his point with two arguments, one positive and the other negative. Positively, if a couple follows Paul's advice and abstains from relations (1 Cor 7:29), they do not cease to be husband and wife; by mutual agreement they restrain the concupiscence of the flesh but not conjugal love. Negatively, a man who commits fornication does not thereby contract marriage, whereas a chaste man and woman are husband and wife "because there is no fleshly intercourse, but only the union of hearts between them."[54]

The sort of vocabulary that Augustine uses in the section that follows[55] demonstrates that what he, like Ambrose, had in mind in

---

[51] Ambrose, *Commentary on Luke* 2, 5 (text 21).

[52] Ambrose, *On the Consecration of a Virgin* 6, 41 (text 23).

[53] Augustine, Sermon 51, 21 (text 38).

[54] Ibid. Augustine's point, that union of hearts constitutes marriage, is parallel to a principle of Roman law on the role of *affectus* or *affectio* in constituting marriage. In classical Roman law, *maritalis affectio* means "the intent to marry." The *Code* of Justinian (5, 17, 11) stated, "Marriages are contracted not by dowries but by affection" ("Non enim dotibus sed affectu matrimonia contrahuntur"; *Corpus Iuris Civilis 2: Codex Iustinianus*, ed. Paul Krüger [Berlin: Weidmann, 1923], 213). On *affectus* as constitutive of marriage see also *Novellae* 22, 3 (ed. Krüger, ibid. 3, 149). See John T. Noonan, "Marital Affection in the Canonists," *Studia Gratiana* 12 (1967): 481-509. Noonan points out that medieval canonists so elaborated their definition of marriage that the marriage of Joseph and Mary could be judged a valid one (ibid., 495-96). On the role of consent in marriage, see also the case that Augustine proposes in *On the Good of Marriage* 5, 5.

[55] Augustine, Sermon 51, 22.

writing about marriage was the juridical understanding of marriage from Roman law. The presence of several terms from Roman juridical language in Sermon 51, 22 points to the source of Augustine's ideas. The terms are: "marriage contract" (*tabulae matrimoniales*), marriage contracted "for the sake of procreating children" (*liberorum procreandorum causa*), and "matrimonial consent" (*matrimoniale pactum*). *Tabulae matrimoniales* and its synonym, *tabulae nuptiales*, designated the marriage contract;[56] the use of such contracts can be traced to the beginning of the Principate. The phrase *liberorum quaerendorum* (or *procreandorum*) *causa* was the juridical definition of the purpose of an authentic Roman marriage.[57] Augustine also writes of the *matrimoniale pactum*;[58] *pactum* or *pactio* was the general juristic term for agreement or consent.[59]

At first glance, the phrase "for the sake of procreating children" (*liberorum procreandorum causa*) may seem to militate against Augustine's contention that marriage is constituted by consent. But his point is that marriage is contracted not to satisfy a man's lust, but for a good external to the couple, namely, children. Augustine is quite dramatic at this place in the sermon. He portrays the moment when a father hands his daughter over to another man:

> The contract is recited, it's read out in the presence of all
> the witnesses, and what's read out is "for the sake of

---

56 See Adolf Berger, *Encyclopedic Dictionary of Roman Law*, Transactions of the American Philosophical Society, new series, vol. 43, part 2 (Philadelphia: American Philosophical Society, 1953), 728-29 (*tabulae nuptiales* or *matrimoniales*). This volume, and the references it contains, have provided the basis for most of the information on Roman law in this paper. In Roman juristic language, *nuptiae* and *matrimonium* are practically synonyms, whereas *coniugium* does not appear to be a juridical term. *Nuptiae* may be the older term, and more related to the wedding ceremony. "The Roman marriage was a factual relation between man and woman . . . based on *affectio maritalis* (intention to be husband and wife). . . ." Ibid., 578.

57 "At the registration of citizens the head of a family was asked whether he was living with a wife *liberorum quaerendorum causa*. Hence a woman married in *iustae nuptiae* = *uxor liberorum quaerendorum causa*." Ibid., 563.

58 Augustine, Sermon 51, 22.

59 The *Digesta* of Justinian stated that *pactum* or *pactio* was "the agreement and consent of two or more persons concerning the same subject." *Digesta* 2, 14, 1, 2 (ed. Mommsen, 1: 62); Berger, *Encyclopedic Dictionary*, 614.

procreating children"; and it's called the matrimonial
contract. Unless this were what wives are given away
and taken for, who with any sense of shame would give
away his daughter to another's lust? But to save parents
from being ashamed when they give away their
daughters, the contract is read out, to make them
fathers-in-law, not whoremongers. So what's read out in
the contract? "For the sake of procreating children." The
father's brow clears, his face is saved when he hears the
words of the contract. Let's consider the face of the man
who is taking a wife. The husband too should be
ashamed to take her on any other terms, if the father is
ashamed to give her away on any other terms.[60]

The teaching that Joseph contracted a true marriage with Mary
was not new to Augustine in Sermon 51. He had proposed it as early as
book 23 of *Against Faustus the Manichee*, written just after he was
ordained a bishop: Joseph was Mary's husband in affection and in the
intercourse of mind. In Christians' faith, the heart of marriage is not
carnal union but the kind of union Christ has with his members.[61]
Augustine presents the same argument in *On the Harmony of the
Gospels*: the relation between married persons can be the affection of
the mind.[62] And in *On Marriage and Concupiscence* he writes that the
designation "wife" is not untrue simply because carnal relations are
absent.[63] Finally, in his first work against Julian of Eclanum, he writes
that what constitutes marriage is the "faith of the betrothal."[64]

---

[60] Augustine, Sermon 51, 22 (trans. Edmund Hill, *Sermons III [51-94] on the New Testament*, Works of Saint Augustine 3, 3 [Brooklyn: New City Press, 1991], 33-34).

[61] Augustine, *Against Faustus the Manichee* 23, 8 (text 29).

[62] Augustine, *On the Harmony of the Gospels* 2, 1, 2 (text 30).

[63] Augustine, *On Marriage and Concupiscence* 1, 11, 12 (text 45).

[64] Augustine, *Against Julian* 5, 12, 48 (text 46). Augustine continues: "He did not think the bond of conjugal faith should be dissolved because the hope of carnal intercourse had been taken away."

In two other works, *On Marriage and Concupiscence* and *Against Julian*, Augustine defined the three goods of marriage: fidelity, which prevents adultery; offspring; and the sacramental bond, because there is no divorce. All three goods, he writes, are fulfilled in the parents of Christ.[65]

Thus Augustine, like Ambrose, by drawing on the understanding of marriage from Roman law, can give an account of the marriage of Mary and Joseph as a true marriage and offer an understanding of marriage that finds its essence in a relationship between two persons rather than in corporeal intercourse. The high point of Augustine's teaching is his assertion that a marriage is constituted by conjugal love (*caritas coniugalis*), an idea that Roman law could never have proposed.

## 4. MAY JOSEPH BE CALLED THE FATHER OF JESUS?

Some Fathers were hesitant to call Joseph "father." Origen calls Joseph Jesus' foster-father,[66] or says he is called father because of his place in the genealogy of Jesus.[67] Epiphanius of Salamis is far more decisive: "Joseph was in the rank of father ... but he was not a father. ... For how could one who did not have relations be his father? This is impossible."[68]

Augustine saw the point differently. He devotes almost one third of Sermon 51 to defending Joseph's true fatherhood of Jesus. Since he clearly affirms Mary's perpetual virginity and thus her virginal conception of Jesus, he proposes an understanding of fatherhood that is not merely physical or corporeal. The essence of fatherhood, he will write, consists not in the act of begetting but rather in a relationship between a man and his son.

---

[65] Augustine, *Against Julian* 5, 12, 46; cf. *On Marriage and Concupiscence* 1, 17, 19.

[66] Origen, *Homilies on Luke* 16, 1 (text 11), *nutricius* in Jerome's Latin.

[67] Ibid. 17, 1 (text 12).

[68] Epiphanius, *Panarion* 51, 10, 7-8 (text 16).

In his affirmation of Joseph's true fatherhood, Augustine begins from Scripture, where Luke twice writes of Joseph as Jesus' father.[69] In Sermon 51, he writes clearly, "As she was in chastity a mother, so was he in chastity a father. Whoever then says that he ought not to be called father, because he did not beget his son in the usual way, looks rather to the satisfaction of passion in the procreation of children, and not the natural feeling of affection. What others desire to fulfill in the flesh, he in a more excellent way fulfilled in the spirit."[70]

To establish his first point, that the act of begetting itself is not the essence of fatherhood, Augustine constructs a kind of gradation or scale of fatherhood.[71] The lowest sort of fatherhood is begetting children outside of marriage, in adultery; these children are called "natural children" (*filii naturales*) and are ranked below the offspring of a lawful marriage, "conjugal children" (*filii coniugales*). In regard to the work of the flesh, the begettings of natural children and of conjugal children are equal. Some other factor must distinguish them, and that factor is chastity, for the love of a wife is more chaste than that of a concubine. Following this scale, there exists a third, higher sort of fatherhood, one from which the work of the flesh is absent: namely, adoption. In this instance a man is a father without begetting his son; or rather, parents who adopt children "beget them chastely in the heart, whom they cannot beget in the flesh."[72] We should consider the laws of adoption, Augustine writes, "the will of the one adopting has more rights over the child than the nature of the one who begets him does."[73] Augustine contrasts nature with will and finds the latter higher in value. Joseph's fatherly relation to Jesus is of this general sort, but higher still, since the "work of the flesh" was wholly absent from the

---

[69] Lk 2:33, 48.

[70] Augustine, Sermon 51, 26 (trans. R. G. MacMullen, *Homilies on the Gospels*, NPNF 1, 6 [rpt. Grand Rapids: Eerdmans, 1974], 255).

[71] Ibid. (text 41).

[72] Ibid.

[73] Ibid.

begetting of Jesus. "For if a man were able to beget children from his wife without intercourse, should he not be more joyful, insofar as she, whom he loves all the more, is more chaste?"[74] he writes.

This argument—admittedly strange to modern perceptions—depends on valuing chastity as a virtue, even within marriage. It is also a way to imagine what, apart from Christian revelation—is unimaginable—fatherhood without intercourse. Augustine's grammar reveals his thought: "if a man were able," *si ... posset*, an unreal condition. The only instance in which such a thing happened was the conception of Jesus. But that conception, Augustine argues, does not deprive Joseph of true fatherhood, because fatherhood comprises far more than begetting. Or rather, there is a spiritual begetting that is superior to physical begetting: "What another man desires to fulfill by the flesh, he fulfilled in a better way, by the spirit."[75]

When he asks what constitutes true fatherhood, Augustine has three answers: paternal authority; natural affection; and marital fidelity, love, and affection. Joseph's paternal authority is demonstrated in the angel's command to him to name the child[76] and in Jesus' subjection to his parents at Nazareth.[77] Secondly, fatherhood is constituted more perfectly by love than by passion. "Whoever says," Augustine writes, "that 'he should not be called a father, because he did not beget a son in that way,' seeks passion (*libido*) and not the feeling of love (*caritatis affectus*) in begetting children."[78] And finally, wedded love is superior to adultery because a true wife is marked by her feelings of fidelity, of wedlock, and of a love more sincere and more chaste.[79]

---

[74] Ibid. (text 41).

[75] Ibid.

[76] Ibid., 29.

[77] Ibid., 30.

[78] Ibid., 26 (text 40); see also 25 (text 39).

[79] Ibid., 26.

## 5. CONCLUSION: THE ROOTS OF DEVOTION TO ST. JOSEPH IN THE EARLY CHURCH

The fifth and last question posed was this: can we speak of devotion to St. Joseph in the early Church? In a word, no. There is no cult of St. Joseph in the early Church; the cult had its hesitant beginnings only around the year 1000. But the roots of such a devotion are older. Like all roots, they are beneath the surface, and thus not readily seen. What the Fathers do is to establish, in bare outline, Joseph's place in the mystery of salvation.

The answers to the two exegetical questions posed earlier cleared the way for doctrinal development. The Fathers taught that Jesus was indeed the Son of David and that the so-called brothers and sisters of Jesus were not children of Mary. Thus the key point about Jesus' ancestry is not Joseph's bloodline but Jesus' Davidic sonship, and the gospels posed no obstacle to affirming that Davidic sonship. And further, the "brothers and sisters of Jesus" were not an obstacle to affirming Mary's perpetual virginity.

Further, doctrinal development followed three points: the gospel's statement that Joseph was a just man, the dignity of the marriage of Joseph and Mary, and Joseph's paternal authority in regard to Jesus. A few examples from the writings of the Fathers will illustrate this development.

Origen, in his *Homilies on Luke*,[80] calls Joseph the "overseer" (*dispensator*, in Jerome's Latin) of Jesus' birth. The Latin word surely represents the Greek *oikonomos*;[81] and the word *oikonomia*, the root meaning of which was the management of a household, designated God's whole plan for the salvation of the world. Thus Origen acknowledges that Joseph had a place in God's plan for the salvation of the world.

John Chrysostom explains at length the meaning of the statement made in Mt 1:19, that Joseph was a just man.[82] Justice, he writes, has a

---

[80] At 13, 7.

[81] Origen has a similar usage in *Against Celsus* 8, 31.

[82] John Chrysostom, *Homilies on Matthew* 4, 7 (text 20).

double sense: freedom from covetousness and universal virtue. The Scripture, he continues, generally uses "justice" in the latter sense, as, for example, of Job, and of Zachary and Elizabeth. Thus Chrysostom assigns Joseph, the just man, the same rank of virtue as these exemplary figures of the Old and New Testaments.

But the highest praise of Joseph comes from Augustine, who rigorously teaches that Joseph may rightly be called both the husband of Mary and the father of Jesus. In both cases, he raises the concepts—of marriage and of fatherhood—above the physical or corporeal to the intellectual or spiritual level. Marriage is constituted by intention, not by intercourse; and fatherhood is established by a relation to the child, not by simple begetting.

In the Middle Ages reflection on St. Joseph continued along the paths set by the Fathers, East and West, until the rise of a true devotion to him in the fifteenth century. In many ways, the Church has continued the legacy of the Fathers, in the liturgy and elsewhere. The most notable example was Pope John XXIII's insertion of the words "and Joseph her husband" ("sed et beati Ioseph, eiusdem virginis sponsi") into the Roman Canon. In contrast, Augustine's contention that Joseph may be called Jesus' father has never been taken up into liturgical language. The preface of St. Joseph and the prayer over the gifts in the votive Mass of St. Joseph speak of his "fatherly care" (*paterna vices*); that is as far as the liturgy goes.

Interest in St. Joseph, and devotion to him, have grown rapidly since the fifteenth century. In elaborating that devotion, however, the Church did not innovate but drew on Scripture and on the traditions about Joseph found in the writings of the Fathers. And perhaps that is the way it ought to be.

# ST. JOSEPH
## IN
# EARLY CHRISTIANITY

DEVOTION AND THEOLOGY

ANTHOLOGY

# PRINCIPAL PASSAGES
# FROM THE FATHERS OF THE CHURCH
# ON ST. JOSEPH

1. Justin Martyr, *Dialogue with Trypho*, 88 (155/65): Joseph a carpenter

When Jesus came to the Jordan, therefore, being considered the son of Joseph the carpenter, and having no comeliness, as the Scriptures affirmed, he was thought to be a carpenter (for, when he was on earth he used to work as a carpenter, making ploughs and yokes, and thereby giving us symbolic lessons of the necessity of leading a just and active life). (Trans. Thomas B. Falls, *Writings of Saint Justin Martyr*, FC 6 [New York, 1948], 289-90.)

2. Hegesippus, quoted by Eusebius, *Ecclesiastical History* 3, 11 (ca. 180): Clopas was Joseph's brother

Then [i.e., after the martyrdom of James] they all discussed together whom they should choose as a fit person to succeed James, and voted unanimously that Symeon, son of the Clopas mentioned in the gospel narrative [Jn 19:25; cf. Lk 24:18], was a fit person to occupy the throne of the Jerusalem see. He was, so it is said, a cousin of the Savior, for Hegesippus tells us that Clopas was Joseph's brother. (Trans. G. A. Williamson, *Eusebius: The History of the Church from Christ to Constantine* [rpt. Minneapolis, 1975], 123-24.)

3. Irenaeus, *Against the Heresies* 3, 22, 4 (180/90): Mary was Joseph's wife

So also Mary, having as her spouse him who had been destined for her in advance [*Maria habens praedestinatum virum*], and being nevertheless a virgin, by her obedience became the cause of salvation both to herself and to the whole human race. And on this account the law terms a woman who is betrothed to a man the wife of him who betrothed her, although she is still a virgin.[83] (SC 211, 440.)

4. Julius Africanus, *Letter to Aristides* (before 240), quoted in Eusebius, *Ecclesiastical History* 1, 7, 5-10: Joseph's ancestors and the levirate law

What I am trying to say will become clear if I explain the interrelation of the families. If we reckon the generations from David through Solomon, we find that the third from the end is Matthan, who begot Jacob, Joseph's father; if we follow Luke and reckon from David's son Nathan, the corresponding third from the end is Melchi, Joseph being the son of Heli, Melchi's son. Joseph then being the subject of our study, I have to explain how each appears in the records as his father, Jacob tracing his descent from Solomon and Heli from Nathan. Before that I must explain how these two, Jacob and Heli, were brothers, and before that how their fathers, Matthan and Melchi, members of different families, are stated to have been Joseph's grandfathers. Well now, Matthan and Melchi, successive husbands of the same wife, fathered half-brothers, for the law allows a woman who has been either divorced or widowed to marry again. The wife in question, whose name is given as Estha, first married Matthan the descendant of Solomon, and bore him Jacob; then on the death of Matthan the widow married Melchi, whose line went back to Nathan, and who belonged to the same tribe, though not to the same family, and by him had a son Heli. Thus though the families were different, we shall find that Jacob and Heli had the same mother. When Heli died childless, his brother Jacob took his wife and by her became the father of Joseph in the third generation. According to nature Joseph was his son—and according to reason, so that Scripture says, "Jacob begot Joseph"; but according to law he was Heli's son; for Jacob as a good brother "raised up" offspring to him. It follows that the genealogy in which he finds a place cannot be invalidated, though Matthew the evangelist in his account says,

---

[83] All translations not otherwise marked are the author's.

"Jacob begot Joseph," whereas Luke says, "Who was, as people imagined"—note this comment—"the son of Joseph, the son of Heli, the son of Melchi." It was impossible to express legal descent more explicitly, and never once from beginning to end did he use the word "begot" with reference to this type of fatherhood, as he traced the line, in the reverse direction, to "Adam, the son of God." (Trans. G. A. Williamson, *Eusebius: The History of the Church from Christ to Constantine* [rpt. Minneapolis, 1975], 54-55.)

5. Celsus, *The True Word* (ca. 178), quoted by Origen (*Against Celsus* 1, 28): Mary committed adultery

After this, he [i.e. Celsus] represents the Jew as having a conversation with Jesus himself and refuting him on many charges, as he thinks: first, because *he fabricated the story of his birth from a virgin*; and he reproaches him because *he came from a Jewish village and from a poor country woman who earned her living by spinning.* He said that *she was driven out by her husband, who was a carpenter by trade, as she was convicted of adultery.* Then he says that *after she had been driven out by her husband and while she was wandering about in a disgraceful way she secretly gave birth to Jesus.* (Trans. Henry Chadwick, *Origen: Contra Celsum* [Cambridge, 1953], 28.)

6. Ibid., quoted by Origen (*Against Celsus* 1, 32): Jesus was the son of the soldier Panthera by adultery

Let us return, however, to the words put into the mouth of the Jew, *where the mother of Jesus* is described as having been *turned out by the carpenter who was betrothed to her, as she had been convicted of adultery and had a child by a certain soldier named Panthera.* Let us consider whether those who fabricated the myth that the virgin and Panthera committed adultery and that the carpenter turned her out, were not blind when they concocted all this to get rid of the miraculous conception by the Holy Spirit. (Trans. ibid., 31-32.)

7. Origen, *Against Celsus* 6, 36 (ca. 246): Jesus was not a carpenter

Furthermore, he [Celsus] did not observe that Jesus himself is not described as a carpenter anywhere in the gospels accepted in the churches.[84] (Trans. ibid., 352.)

8. Origen, *Homilies on Luke* 6, 3-4 (ca. 239/42): why Mary was betrothed to Joseph

Scripture then relates that, six months after Elizabeth conceived, "the angel Gabriel was sent by God to a town of Galilee named Nazareth, to a virgin betrothed to a man named Joseph of the house of David, and the virgin's name was Mary" [Lk 1:26-27]. Again I turn the matter over in my mind and ask why, when God had decided that the Savior should be born of a virgin, he chose not a girl who was not betrothed, but precisely one who was already betrothed. Unless I am mistaken, this is the reason. The Savior ought to be born of a virgin who was not only betrothed but, as Matthew writes, had already been given to her husband, although he had not yet had relations with her [cf. Mt 1:24]. Otherwise, if the virgin were seen growing big with a child, the state of virginity itself would be a cause of disgrace.

I found an elegant statement in the letter of a martyr—I mean Ignatius, the second bishop of Antioch after Peter. During a persecution, he fought against wild animals at Rome. He stated: "Mary's virginity escaped the notice of the ruler of this age."[85] It escaped his notice because of Joseph, and because of their wedding, and because Mary was thought to have a husband. If she had not been betrothed or had (as people thought) a husband, her virginity could never have been concealed from the "ruler of this age" [1 Cor 2:6; Jn 12:31]. Immediately a silent thought would have occurred to the devil: "How can this woman, who has not slept with a man, be pregnant? This

[84] Origen read Mk 6:3 ("Is this not the carpenter?") in a form assimilated to Mt 13:55 ("Is this not the carpenter's son?"), as many ancient authorities did; see the critical apparatus of the New Testament.

[85] Ignatius of Antioch, *Ephesians* 19, 1.

conception must be divine. It must be something more sublime than human nature." But the Savior had so arranged his plan that the devil did not know he had taken on a body. When he was conceived, he escaped the devil's notice. Later he commanded his disciples "not to make him known" [Mt 12:16]. (Trans. Joseph T. Lienhard, *Origen: Homilies on Luke, Fragments on Luke*, FC 94 [Washington, 1996], 24-25.)

9. Ibid. 7, 4: heretics' calumnies

Therefore "the infant in [Elizabeth's] womb leapt, and she was filled with the Holy Spirit. She cried out in a loud voice and said, 'Blessed are you among women'" [Lk 1:41-42]. At this point we ought to refute the heretics' usual objections;[86] otherwise some simpler people might be deceived. Someone or other gave vent to his madness and claimed that the Savior had repudiated Mary because she had been joined to Joseph after his birth [cf. Mt 1:25; 12:48]. This is what he said. I hope he knows what the state of his mind was when he said it. If heretics ever raise an objection like this to you, answer them and say, "Elizabeth surely was filled with the Holy Spirit when she said, 'Blessed are you among women' [Lk 1:42]. If the Holy Spirit called Mary 'blessed,' how could the Savior repudiate her?" Furthermore, they assert that Mary had marital relations after the birth of Jesus. But they have no source of proof. For the children who were called Joseph's[87] were not born of Mary. There is no passage in Scripture that mentions this. (Trans. ibid., 29-30.)

10. Ibid. 13, 7: Joseph the "overseer"

The passage continues: "And it happened that when the angels had left them and returned to heaven, the shepherds said to one another, 'Let us go over to Bethlehem and see this word that has been done, which the Lord revealed to us.' And they hastened and went,

[86] The identity of these heretics is uncertain.

[87] Cf. Mt 13:55, and Origen, *Commentary on Matthew* 10, 17 (text 15).

and they found Mary and Joseph and the child" [Lk 2:15-16]. They
hastened—not cautiously, not at a slow pace—and they went. Thus
they found Joseph, the overseer[88] of the Lord's birth, and Mary, who
bore Jesus in childbirth, and the Savior himself, "lying in a manger"
[Lk 2:16]. That was the manger of which the inspired prophet said,
"The ox knows his owner and the ass his master's manger" [Is 1:3].[89]
(Trans. ibid., 55.)

## 11. Ibid. 16, 1: Joseph called Jesus' father

The Gospel says, "And his father and mother were astonished at
these things that were being said about him" [Lk 2:33]. Let us gather
into one those things that were said and written about Jesus at his
birth. Then we shall be able to know the single points, each of which
merits our astonishment. Wherefore both his father—for Joseph has
also been called this because he was his foster-father—and his mother
were astonished at all that was being said about him. (Trans. ibid., 65.)

## 12. Ibid. 17, 1: why Luke calls Joseph Jesus' father

It is Luke who wrote, "The Holy Spirit will come upon you, and
the power of the Most High will overshadow you. For this reason what
will be born is holy. He will be called the Son of God" [Lk 1:35]. He
clearly handed down to us that Jesus was the son of a virgin, and was
not conceived by human seed. But Luke has also attested that Joseph
was his father when he said, "And his father and mother were astonished by the things that were said about him" [Lk 2:33]. Therefore,
what reason was there that Luke should call him a father when he was
not a father? Anyone who is content with a simple explanation will
say, "The Holy Spirit honored Joseph with the name of 'father' because
he had reared Jesus." But one who looks for a more profound expla-

---

[88] Origen's term (dispensator, in Jerome's Latin, representing the Greek oikonomos),
suggests Joseph's role in the divine economy of salvation.

[89] Origen, at this place, is the first Christian writer to mention the ox and the ass in the
stable at Bethlehem.

nation can say that the Lord's genealogy extends from David to Joseph. Lest the naming of Joseph, who was not the Savior's father, should appear to be pointless, he is called the Lord's "father," to give him his place in the genealogy.[90] (Trans. ibid., 70.)

13. Ibid. 20, 4-5: Joseph's and Mary's faith was not yet perfect; Jesus' subjection to Joseph

At the same time, pay attention to this also. As long as he was in his Father's domain, he was above. Joseph and Mary did not yet have perfect faith. For this reason, they were unable to remain above with him. Scripture says that he went down with them. Jesus frequently goes down with his disciples. He does not always stay on a mountain. He does not always keep to the heights. He is on the mountain with Peter, James, and John, but with the rest of the disciples he is in another place. Because those who were troubled with various diseases were not strong enough to climb to the mountain, he "went down and came" [Mt 8:1]. to those who were below. Here too Scripture says, "He went down with them and came to Nazareth, and was subject to them" [Lk 2:51].

Children, we should learn to be subject to our parents. The greater is subject to the lesser. Jesus understood that Joseph was greater than he in age, and therefore he gave him the honor due a parent. He gave an example to every son. Sons should be subject to their fathers; and, if they have no fathers, they should be subject to those who are as old as fathers. But why am I speaking about parents and children? If Jesus, the Son of God, is subject to Joseph and Mary, shall I not be subject to the bishop? God appointed him a father to me. Shall I not be subject to the presbyter, whom the Lord's choice set over me? I think Joseph understood that Jesus, who was subject to him, was greater than he. He knew that the one subject to him was greater than he and, out of reverence, restrained his authority. So each one should realize that often a lesser

---

[90] Origen believed that Luke named Joseph in the genealogy of Jesus to establish Jesus' Davidic descent. Cf. *Commentary on Romans* 1, 5.

man is put in charge of better men. Sometimes it happens that he who is subject is better than he who appears to be in authority. Once someone who enjoys a higher position understands this, he will not be lifted up in pride by the fact that he is greater. He will know that a better one is subject to himself, just as Jesus was subject to Joseph. (Trans. ibid., 85-86.)

14. Ibid. 28, 3: Jesus' double genealogy

But, when he rises up from the washing and his ancestry is described for a second time, he is born not through Solomon but through Nathan.[91] Nathan reproached his father for the death of Uriah and the birth of Solomon. But in Matthew the word "begot" is always added, whereas Luke is completely silent on the matter. In Matthew it is written, "Abraham begot Isaac; Isaac begot Jacob; Jacob begot Judah and his brothers; Judah begot Perez and Zerah by Tamar" [Mt 1:2-3]. Right up to the end "begot" is always added. But in Luke, when Jesus comes up from baptism, the passage says, "The son, as it was believed, of Joseph" [Lk 3:23]. And in such a long series of names the word for "begetting" is never recorded, except that "he was thought to be the son of Joseph." (Trans. ibid., 116.)

15. Origen, *Commentary on Matthew* 10, 17 (ca. 244): Joseph's children by a previous marriage; Joseph not a virgin

They thought, then, that he was the son of Joseph and Mary. But some say, basing it on a tradition in the *Gospel according to Peter*, as it is entitled, or the *Book of James*, that the brethren of Jesus were sons of Joseph by a former wife, whom he married before Mary. Now those who say so wish to preserve the honor of Mary in virginity to the end, so that body of hers, which was appointed to minister to the Word that said, 'The Holy Spirit shall come upon you, and the power of the Most High shall overshadow you' [Lk 1:5], might not know intercourse with

---

[91] Origen here erroneously identifies the Nathan who, according to Lk 3:31, was David's son, with the prophet Nathan, and refers to 2 Sam 12.

a man after the Holy Spirit came into her and the power from on high overshadowed her. And I think it in harmony with reason that Jesus was the first fruit among men of the purity that consists in chastity, and Mary among women; for it would not be pious to ascribe to any other than to her the first fruit of virginity. (Trans. John Patrick, ANF 10 [rpt. Grand Rapids, 1974], 424.[92])

16. Epiphanius of Salamis, *Panarion* 51, 10, 7-8 (377): Joseph was not Jesus' father

Joseph was in the rank of father … but he was not a father. … For how could one who did not have relations be his father? This is impossible. (GCS Epiphanius 2, 262.)

17. Jerome, *Against Helvidius* 19 (383): defends Joseph's virginity

But just as we do not deny these statements that have been written down, so also, by the same token, we do deny those things that have not been written down. We believe that God was born of a virgin, because we have read such a statement. We do not believe that Mary married after she brought forth her son, because we have not read such a statement. We are not saying this in order to condemn marriage; virginity itself, to be sure, is the fruit of marriage; but because it is not right for us to make rash judgments about holy men. For if we base our judgment on probability, we can argue that Joseph had many wives, because Abraham had many wives, because Jacob had many wives; and that the brothers of the Lord were born of these wives, as many imagine is the case, based not so much on a pious as on a brazen rashness. You can say that Mary did not remain a virgin; as for me, I claim more emphatically that Joseph himself was also a virgin through Mary, so that a virgin son might be born of a virgin wedlock. For if fornication ill befits a holy man, and it is not written down that he had a second wife, but was the guardian rather than the husband of Mary

---

[92] This and other translations from the series Ante-Nicene Fathers, and Nicene and Post-Nicene Fathers, have been altered slightly to eliminate outdated expressions.

whom he supposedly possessed as his own, the conclusion follows that he, who was deemed worthy to be called the father of the Lord, remained a virgin with Mary. (Trans. John N. Hritzu, *Saint Jerome: Dogmatic and Polemical Works*, FC 53 [Washington, 1965], 38-39.)

18. Jerome, *Commentary on Matthew* 1, on Mt 1:18 (398): genealogy through Joseph; Joseph and Mary related

The careful reader might inquire and say, "Since Joseph was not the father of our Lord and Savior, how does it pertain to the Lord that the order of generations is traced to Joseph?" To him we respond: first, it is not the custom of Scripture to include women in the order of generations; and secondly Joseph and Mary were from one tribe, since by the law he had to take her, as a relative, and, at the same time, they were enrolled at Bethlehem as people born of one lineage. (CCL 77, 10.)

19. Ibid. 2, on Mt 12:49-50: brethren of the Lord are not Joseph's children

Certain people who follow the ravings of the apocrypha assume that the brethren of the Lord are sons of Joseph from another wife and invent a certain woman, Melcha or Escha. But we, as we maintained in the book that we wrote against Helvidius, understand as brethren of the Lord not the sons of Joseph but the cousins (*consobrini*) of the Savior, children of Mary, the Lord's maternal aunt (*matertera*), who is said to be the mother of James the Less and Joseph and Jude, who, as we read in another passage in the gospel, were called brethren of the Lord. Indeed, all scripture shows that cousins are called brethren. (CCL 77, 100-101.)

20. John Chrysostom, *Homilies on Matthew* 4, 7, on Mt 1:19 (390): Joseph the just man

He [Matthew] introduces Joseph as contributing, by what he underwent, to the proof of the things mentioned; and by his narrative all but says, "If you doubt me, and if you suspect my testimony, believe her husband." For "Joseph," says he, "her husband, being a just man." By "a just man" in this place he means him who is virtuous in all things. For both freedom from covetousness is justice, and universal virtue is also justice; and it is mostly in this latter sense that the Scripture uses the name of justice; as when it says, "a man who was just and true" [Job 1:1]; and again, "they were both just" [Lk 1:6]. Being then "just," that is good and considerate, "he was minded to put her away privately." For this intent he tells what took place before Joseph's being fully informed, that you might not mistrust what was done after he knew.

However, such a one was not liable to be made a public example only, but that she should also be punished was the command of the law. Whereas Joseph remitted not only that greater punishment, but the less likewise, namely, the disgrace. For so far from punishing, he was not minded even to make an example of her. You see a man under self-restraint, and freed from the most tyrannical of passions. For you know how great a thing jealousy is: and therefore he said, to whom these things are clearly known, "for full of jealousy is the rage of a husband" [Prov 6:34]; "he will not spare in the day of vengeance"; and "jealousy is cruel as the grave" [Cant 8:6]. And we know too of many that have chosen to give up their lives rather than fall under the suspicion of jealousy. But in this case it was not so little as suspicion, the burden of the womb entirely convicting her. But nevertheless he was so free from passion as to be unwilling to grieve the virgin even in the least matters. Thus, whereas to keep her in his house seemed like a transgression of the law, but to expose and bring her to trial would constrain him to deliver her to die; he does none of these things, but conducts himself now by a higher rule than the law. (Trans. George Prevost, NPNF 1, 10, 23.)

21. Ambrose, *Commentary on Luke* 2, 5 (ca. 390): Joseph's marriage a true marriage

The fact that Scripture often calls her a wife should not disturb you. For it is not the loss of virginity but the solemn affirming of the marriage (*coniugii testificatio*) and the celebration of the wedding (*nuptiarum celebratio*) that is being stated thereby. Then too, no one puts away a woman whom he has not accepted, and thus he who wanted to put her away admitted that he had accepted her. (SC 45, 74.)

22. Ibid. 3, 3-4: the genealogy of Joseph; Joseph and Mary were related

But why is the genealogy of Joseph rather than that of Mary recorded, although Mary bore Christ by the Holy Spirit and Joseph appears absent from the Lord's generation? We might have doubts, unless the custom of the Scriptures instructed us: for it always looks for the genealogy of the husband. ... For the identity of the husband is sought, who even in the senate and the other councils of cities sustains the dignity of the family. How deformed it would be, however, if the genealogy of the husband were ignored and the genealogy of the woman sought out, so that he, who was to be proclaimed to the peoples of the whole world, should seem not to have had a father! ...

Do not be amazed, if Matthew goes through the order of generations from Abraham to Joseph, but Luke does so from Joseph to Adam and God. Do not be amazed that the genealogy of Joseph is recorded. For he who was born in the flesh ought to have followed the usages of the flesh, and he who came into the world ought to be described according to the world's customs, especially since Mary's genealogy is also found in Joseph's. For since Joseph was the just man, he took a wife of his tribe and his kinship, and a just man could not act against what the law had prescribed. ... Thus at the time of the census Joseph, of the house and city of David, went up to register with Mary his wife. She registers in the same house and the same city, and shows that she is of the same tribe and the same city. (SC 45, 120-21.)

23. Ambrose, *On the Consecration of a Virgin* 6, 41 (392): the essence of marriage

The verse that reads, "Joseph took his wife and set out for Egypt" should not affect the argument, for a woman espoused to a man received the name of "wife" (*coniunx*). For when a marriage is initiated,[93] the name of "marriage" (*coniugium*) is employed. For the loss of virginity (*defloratio virginitatis*) does not make a marriage, but rather the marital agreement (*pactio coniugalis*). In short, there exists a marriage (*coniugium*) when a young girl is wed, ("cum iungitur puella, coniugium est"), not when she is known by relations with her husband. (PL 16, 330C-331A.)

24. Ibid. 6, 43: the meaning of "brethren"

The Lord himself teaches that "brethren" names a relationship of a tribe or a nation or a people. For he says, "I will tell your name to my brethren; in the midst of the Church I will praise you" [Ps 22:22]. Paul too says, "I hoped to be accursed for my brethren" [Rom 9:13]. But the "brethren" could be from Joseph, not from Mary. If anyone pursues this point more carefully, he will discover [an answer]. We have not thought it worth pursuing, because the name of "brother" is clearly common to many groups. (PL 16, 331A-B.)

25. Hilary, *Commentary on Matthew* 1, 3 (398): Joseph's marriage not a true marriage

Because she was betrothed, she is received as a wife. She is 'known' as such after her childbirth—that is, she advances to receive the name 'wife.' She is 'known' [as wife], but she has no relations [with Joseph]. ... Whenever there is a question of these two [that is, Jesus and Joseph], she is called rather the mother of Christ [cf. Mt 2:13, 20; Lk 2:33], because that she was, not the wife of Joseph, for that she was not. ... Therefore, the betrothed also received the name of wife, and

---

[93] Latin *initiare*, "to admit with introductory rites."

after the childbirth, having been recognized as wife, she is presented only as the mother of Jesus. (SC 254, 96.)

26. Ibid. 1, 4: the Lord's brothers were Joseph's sons, not Mary's

But from this passage depraved men presume the authority of their opinion, that our Lord is said to have had several brothers. If they had been sons of Mary, and not rather of Joseph from a previous marriage, the Lord would never have given her over to John the Apostle as his mother at the time of his passion, when he said to both of them, "Woman, behold your son" and "Behold your mother" [Jn 18:26-27], unless, to console her solitude, he left his love as a son to his disciple. (SC 254, 96-98.)

27. Augustine, *Exposition of the Epistle to the Galatians* 8, 5 (394/95): James the "brother" of the Lord

"But I did not see any other apostle except James the brother of the Lord" [Gal 1:19]. James the brother of the Lord should be taken either as one of the sons of Joseph from another wife or as one of the relations of Mary his mother. (CSEL 84, 63.)

28. Augustine, *Against Faustus the Manichee* 3, 3 (397/400): Joseph was adopted

The whole question is how Joseph had two fathers. Supposing this possible, both genealogies may be correct. With two fathers, why not two grandfathers, and so on, up to David, who was the father both of Solomon, who is mentioned in Matthew's list, and of Nathan, who occurs in Luke? This is the difficulty with many people who think it impossible that two men should have one and the same son, forgetting the very obvious fact that a man may be called the son of the person who adopted him as well as of the person who begot him. (Trans. Richard Stothert, NPNF 1, 4, 159.)

29. Ibid. 23, 8: Joseph in the genealogy of Jesus

This assailant of the holy Gospel need find no difficulty in the fact that Christ is called the Son of David, though he was born of a virgin, and though Joseph was not his real father; while the genealogy is brought down by the evangelist Matthew, not to Mary, but to Joseph. First of all, the husband, as the man, is the more honorable; and Joseph was Mary's husband, though she did not live with him, for Matthew himself mentions that she was called Joseph's wife by the angel; as it is also from Matthew that we learn that Mary conceived not by Joseph, but by the Holy Spirit. But if this, instead of being a true narrative written by Matthew the apostle, was a false narrative written by someone else under his name, is it likely that he would have contradicted himself in such an apparent manner, and in passages so immediately connected, as to speak of the Son of David born of Mary without conjugal intercourse, and then, in giving his genealogy, to bring it down to the very man with whom the Virgin is expressly said not to have had intercourse, unless he had some reason for doing so? Even supposing that there were two writers, one calling Christ the Son of David, and giving an account of Christ's progenitors from David down to Joseph; while the other does not call Christ the Son of David, and says that he was born of the Virgin Mary without intercourse with any man; those statements are not irreconcilable, so as to prove that one or both writers must be false. It will appear on reflection that both accounts might be true; for Joseph might be called the husband of Mary, though she was his wife only in affection, and in the intercourse of the mind, which is more intimate than that of the body. In this way it might be proper that the husband of the virgin-mother of Christ should have a place in the list of Christ's ancestors. It might also be the case that some of David's blood flowed in Mary herself, so that the flesh of Christ, although produced from a virgin, still owed its origin to David's seed. But as, in fact, both statements are made by one and the same writer, who informs us both that Joseph was the husband of Mary and that the mother of Christ was a virgin, and that Christ was of the seed of David, and that Joseph is in the list of Christ's progenitors in the line of David, those who prefer the authority of the sacred Gospel to that of heretical fiction must conclude that Mary was not unconnected with the family of David, and that she was properly called the wife of Joseph, because being a woman she was in spiritual alliance with him, though there was no bodily connection. Joseph, too, it is plain, could not be omitted in the genealogy; for, from the superiority of his sex, such an omission would be equivalent to a denial of his relation to the woman with whom he was inwardly united; and believers in Christ are taught not to think carnal connection the chief thing in marriage, as if without this they could not be man and wife, but to imitate in Christian wedlock as closely as possible the parents of Christ, that so they may have the more intimate union with the members of Christ. (Trans. ibid., 315.)

30. Augustine, *On the Harmony* of the Gospels 2, 1, 2 (399/400 or 403/5): the essence of marriage is commitment

Matthew therefore traces out the human generation of Christ, mentioning his ancestors from Abraham downwards, and carrying them on to Joseph the husband of Mary, of whom Jesus was born. For it was not held allowable to consider him dissociated from the married estate that was entered into with Mary, on the ground that she gave birth to Christ, not as the wedded wife of Joseph, but as a virgin. For by this example an illustrious recommendation is made to faithful married persons of the principle, that even when by common consent they maintain their continence, the relation can still remain, and can still be called one of wedlock, inasmuch as, although there is no connection between the sexes of the body, there is the keeping of the affections of the mind; particularly so for this reason, that in their case we see how the birth of a son was a possibility apart from anything of that carnal intercourse that is to be practiced with the purpose of the procreation of children only. (Trans. S. D. F. Salmond, NPNF 1, 6, 102.)

31. Ibid. 2, 2, 4: Mary and Joseph both of Davidic descent

Thus, too, even if one were able to demonstrate that no descent, according to the laws of blood, could be claimed from David for Mary, we should have warrant enough to hold Christ to be the son of David, on the ground of that same mode of reckoning by which also Joseph is called his father. But seeing that the apostle Paul unmistakably tells us that "Christ was of the seed of David according to the flesh" [Rom 1:3], how much more ought we to accept without hesitation the position that Mary herself was also descended in some way, according to the laws of blood, from the lineage of David? (Trans. ibid., 103.)

32. Ibid. 2, 3, 5: Joseph was adopted

Thus, too, we can understand how Luke, in the genealogy contained in his gospel, has named a father for Joseph, not in the person of the father by whom he was begotten, but in that of the father by whom he was adopted, tracing the list of the progenitors upwards until David is reached. (Trans. ibid., 104.)

33. Augustine, *On the Work of Monks* 13, 14 (ca. 400): Joseph was a carpenter, and a virgin

If persons should suggest the Jews [for examples of men who worked at honest labor], their patriarchs tended flocks; if the Greeks whom we call pagans, they considered cobblers quite respectable philosophers; if the Church of God, that just man, chosen to be an example of conjugal and perpetual virginity ["homo ille iustus et ad testimonium coniugalis semper mansurae virginitatis electus"] to whom the Virgin Mary who bore Christ was espoused, was a carpenter. (Trans. Mary Sarah Muldowney, *Saint Augustine: Treatises on Various Subjects*, FC 16 [New York, 1952], 354.)

### 34. Augustine, Sermon 51, 9 (418): Joseph the just man

[On Mt 1:19] The husband was indeed in trouble, but as being a just man he deals not severely; for so great justice is ascribed to this man, as that he neither wished to keep an adulterous wife, nor could bring himself to punish and expose her. "He was minded to put her away privately," because he was not only unwilling to punish, but even to betray her; and mark his genuine justice; for he did not wish to spare her, because he had a desire to keep her; for many spare their adulterous wives through a carnal love, choosing to keep them even though adulterous, that they may enjoy them through a carnal desire. But this just man has no wish to keep her, and so does not love in any carnal sort; and yet he does not wish to punish her; and so in his mercy he spares her. How truly just a man is this! He would neither keep an adulteress, lest he should seem to spare her because of an impure affection, and yet he would not punish or betray her. Deservedly indeed was he chosen for the witness of his wife's virginity: and so he who was in trouble through human infirmity, was assured by divine authority. (Trans. R. G. MacMullen, NPNF 1, 6, 248.)

### 35. Ibid. 16: Joseph a true father

[That the generations of Christ are counted through Joseph.] Now the Scripture is intent on showing that he was not born of Joseph's seed, when he is told in his trouble as to her being with child, "He is of the Holy Ghost"; and yet his paternal authority is not taken from him, forasmuch as he is commanded to name the child; and again the Virgin Mary herself, who was well aware that it was not by him that she conceived Christ, yet calls him the father of Christ. (Trans. ibid., 251.)

### 36. Ibid. 19: Jesus subject to his parents

[On Lk 2:49] The answer then of the Lord Jesus Christ, "I must be about my Father's service," does not in such sense declare God to be his Father, as to deny that Joseph was his father also. ... "He came to Nazareth and was subject to them." It did not say, "He was subject to his mother," or was "subject to her," but "He was subject to them." To whom was he subject? Was it not to his parents? It was to both his parents that he was subject, by the same condescension by which he was the Son of Man. (Trans. ibid., 252.)

37. Ibid. 20: Joseph and Mary were Jesus' parents in time

They were his parents in time, God was his father eternally. They were the parents of the Son of Man. (Trans. ibid.)

38. Ibid. 21: Joseph's marriage was a true marriage

Joseph then was not the less his father, because he knew not the mother of our Lord, as though concupiscence and not conjugal affection (*caritas coniugalis*) constitutes the marriage bond. ...

Are they then not married people who thus live, not requiring from each other any carnal gratification, or exacting the satisfaction of any bodily desire? And yet the wife is subject to the husband, because it is fitting that she should be, and so much the more in subjection is she, in proportion to her greater chastity; and the husband for his part loves his wife truly, as it is written, "in honor and sanctification" [1 Th 4:4], as a coheir of grace: as "Christ," says the Apostle, "loved the Church" [Eph 5:25]. If then this be a union, and a marriage; if it be not the less a marriage because nothing of that kind passes between them, which even with unmarried persons may take place, but then unlawfully; (O that all could live so, but many have not the power!) let them at least not separate those who have the power, and deny that the man is a husband or the woman a wife, because there is no fleshly intercourse, but only the union of hearts between them. (Trans. ibid., 252-53.)

39. Ibid. 25: Joseph was truly Jesus' father

So then was Joseph not a father because he had gotten a son without any lust of the flesh? God forbid that Christian chastity should entertain a thought, which even Jewish chastity entertained not! (Trans. ibid., 254.)

40. Ibid. 26: Joseph a father in chastity

As that then was a true marriage, and a marriage free from all
corruption, so why should not the husband chastely receive what his
wife had chastely brought forth? For as she was a wife in chastity, so was
he in chastity a husband; and as she was in chastity a mother, so was he
in chastity a father. Whoever then says that he ought not to be called
father, because he did not beget his son in the usual way, looks rather to
the satisfaction of passion in the procreation of children, and not the
natural feeling of affection. What others desire to fulfill in the flesh, he
in a more excellent way fulfilled in the spirit. (Trans. ibid., 255.)

41. Ibid.: Joseph was a most excellent father

Not only then must Joseph be a father, but in a most excellent
manner a father. For men beget children of women also who are not
their wives, and they are called natural children, and the children of
the lawful marriage are placed above them. Now as to the manner of
their birth, they are born alike; why then are the latter set above the
other, but because of the love of a wife, of whom children are born, is
the more pure? The union of the sexes is not regarded in this case, for
this is the same in both women. Where has the wife the preeminence
but in her fidelity, her wedded love, her more true and pure affection? If
then a man could have children by his wife without this intercourse,
should he not have so much the more joy thereby, in proportion to the
greater chastity of her whom he loves the most? (Trans. ibid.)

42. Ibid. 27: Joseph was adopted

If one man then can have two fathers, Joseph could have two
fathers also; he might be begotten by one, and adopted by another.
And if this be so, what do their cavilings mean, who insist that
Matthew has followed one set of generations, and Luke another? And
in fact we find that so it is, for Matthew has given Jacob as the father
of Joseph, and Luke Heli. Now it is true it might seem as if one and
the same man, whose son Joseph was, had two names. But inasmuch as

the grandfathers, and all the other progenitors whom they enumerate, are different, and in the very number of the generations, the one has more, and the other fewer, Joseph is plainly shown hereby to have had two fathers. Now having disposed of the cavil of this question, forasmuch as clear reason has shown that it may happen that he who has begotten a child may be one father, and he who has adopted him another: supposing two fathers, it is nothing strange if the grandfathers and the great grandfathers, and the rest in the line upwards who are enumerated, should be different as coming from different fathers. (Trans. ibid.)

43. Ibid. 28: Joseph was adopted

And he [the objector] may, without any opposition from me, refuse to call Joseph adopted, provided he grant that he may have been the son of a man of whose body he was not born. (Trans. ibid., 256.)

44. Ibid. 31: the double genealogy: descent into sin, ascent to expiation

Matthew descends through his generations, to signify our Lord Jesus Christ descending to bear our sins, that in the seed of Abraham all nations might be blessed. ... But Luke reckons in an ascending order, and does not begin to enumerate the generations from the beginning of the account of our Lord's birth, but from that place, where he relates his baptism by John. Now, as in the incarnation of the Lord, the sins of the human race are taken upon him to be borne, so in the consecration of his baptism are they taken on him to be expiated. Accordingly, St. Matthew, as representing his descent to bear our sins, enumerates the generations in a descending order; but the other, as representing the expiation of sins, not his own, of course, but our sins, enumerates them in an ascending order. (Trans. ibid., 257.)

45. Augustine, On Marriage and Concupiscence 1, 11, 12 (418/19): Mary is Joseph's wife

She is called his wife because of her first troth of betrothal, although he had had no carnal knowledge of her, nor was destined to have. The designation of wife was neither destroyed nor made untrue, where there never had been, nor was meant to be, any carnal connection. ... And because of this conjugal fidelity they are both deservedly called "parents" of Christ (not only she as his mother, but he as his father, as being her husband), both having been such in mind and purpose, though not in the flesh. ...

Now, since she bore him without his engendering, they could not surely have both been his parents, of that form of a servant, if they had not been conjugally united, though without carnal connection. Accordingly the genealogical series (although both parents of Christ are mentioned together in the succession) had to be extended, as it is in fact, down rather to Joseph's name, that no wrong might be done, in the case of this marriage, to the male, and indeed the stronger sex, while at the same time there was nothing detrimental to truth, since Joseph, no less than Mary, was of the seed of David, of whom it was foretold that Christ should come. (Trans. Peter Holmes, NPNF 1, 5, 268-69.)

46. Augustine, *Against Julian* 5, 12, 47-48 (422): Joseph was truly Mary's husband

You [i.e. Julian] say, "It was only the common opinion that Joseph was her husband." You would have us think Scripture was merely giving an opinion, not a fact, when it said that the Virgin Mary was his wife. ... What was the purpose of listing the generations up to Joseph, if not because the male sex has the place of honor in marriage? You were afraid to meet this argument in the book you are answering. The evangelist Luke says of our Lord, "Being, as was supposed, the son of Joseph"; because it was so supposed in order that it might be thought he was really begotten through the marriage union of Joseph. Luke wished to remove this false opinion, not to deny, contrary to the angel's testimony, that Mary was Joseph's wife.

You yourself admit that "he received the name of husband from the faith of the betrothal." This faith certainly remained inviolate. When he saw the holy virgin already fruitful with the divine gift, he did not seek another wife, although he would never have sought the virgin herself if she had not needed a husband. He did not think the bond of conjugal faith should be dissolved because the hope of carnal intercourse had been taken away. (Trans. Matthew A. Schumacher, *Saint Augustine: Against Julian*, FC 35 [New York, 1957], 288-89.)

47. Augustine, *Retractations* 33, 2 (=2, 7, 2) (427): Augustine, at the end of his life, accepts Julius Africanus's explanation of the double genealogy

In the third book [of the work *Against Faustus the Manichee*], then, when I was solving the question of how it was possible for Joseph to have two fathers, I, indeed, said that "he was begotten by one and adopted by the other." But I should have mentioned, too, the kind of adoption; for what I said sounds as if another living father had adopted him. The Law, however, also adopted the children of the deceased by ordering that "a brother marry the wife" of his childless, deceased brother and "raise up seed" by the same woman "for his deceased brother" [Dt 25:5]. This explanation of this matter of the two fathers of one man is, indeed, made clearer. The brothers, moreover, were uterine; it happened, in their case, that the other brother, that is, Jacob, by whom Matthew says Joseph was begotten, married the wife of his deceased brother who was called Heli; but he begot him for his own uterine brother whose son, Luke says, was Joseph, certainly not begotten, but adopted according to the Law. This explanation was found in the writings of those who, after the Ascension of the Lord while the memory of it was recent, wrote on this subject. For, in truth, Africanus even mentioned the name of the very woman who gave birth to Jacob, the father of Joseph, by a former husband, Mathan, who was the father of Jacob, the grandfather of Joseph, according to Matthew, and by a second husband, Melchi gave birth to Heli of whom Joseph was the adopted son. I had not, indeed, read this when I replied to Faustus, but, yet, I could not doubt that it was possible for one man through adoption to have two fathers. (Trans. Mary Inez Bogan, *Saint Augustine: The Retractations*, FC 60 [Washington, 1968], 133-34.)

48. Sozomen, *Ecclesiastical History* 6, 2 (439/50): Joseph the carpenter

When Julian [the Apostate] was preparing to enter upon the war against the Persians, he threatened that on the termination of the war he would treat the Christians with severity, and boasted that the Son of the Carpenter would be unable to aid them; the ecclesiastic above mentioned [i.e. Didymus of Alexandria] thereupon rejoined, that the Son of the Carpenter was then preparing him a wooden coffin in view of his death. (Trans. Chester D. Hartranft, *Socrates, Sozomen: Church Histories*, NPNF 2, 2 [rpt. Grand Rapids, 1973], 347.)

49. Pseudo-Augustine, Sermon 195, 6 (6th c., North Africa): Joseph a virgin

Preserve, O Joseph, together with Mary your wife, the mutual virginity of your members; for out of virginal members is begotten the Power of the angels. Let Mary be the spouse of Christ by preserving the virginity of her flesh. You, however, are to be the father of Christ by safeguarding her chastity and revering her virginity. (PL 39, 2110.)

50. Pseudo-Origen, *Homily 17: On the Vigil of the Lord's Nativity* (6th c., perhaps northern Italy): Mary and Joseph did not contract a true marriage

Even though [Mary] is named your wife and "espoused to you," she is not your wife but rather the chosen mother of the only-begotten God … and I will show you later that she may not be held as your wife according to the usage of marriage nor may he who will be born be considered your son. … Wherefore, Joseph, minister to, serve, guard, be watchful, look both to him who is born and to her who gives birth. (GCS Origenes 12, 242.)

# ABBREVIATIONS

ANF     Ante-Nicene Fathers

CCL     *Corpus Christianorum, Series Latina*

CSEL    *Corpus Scriptorum Ecclesiasticorum Latinorum*

FC      Fathers of the Church

GCS     *Die griechischen christlichen Schriftsteller der ersten Jahrhunderte*

NPNF    Nicene and Post-Nicene Fathers

PL      *Patrologia Latina*

RE      *Realenzyklopädie der klassischen Altertumswissenschaft*

SC      *Sources chrétiennes*

# BIBLIOGRAPHY

Albertario, Emilio. "Honor matrimonii e affectio maritalis." Idem, *Studi di diritto romano.* Vol. 1. Milan: A. Giuffrè, 1932.

Augustine, St. *Sermon 51.* Trans. Edmund Hill. *Augustine: Sermons III (51-94) on the New Testament.* The Works of Saint Augustine, 3, 3. Pp. 19-49. Brooklyn: New City Press, 1991.

Augustine, St. *Sermon 51.* Trans. R. G. MacMullen. *Saint Augustin: Sermon on the Mount, Harmony of the Gospels, Homilies on the Gospels.* Nicene and Post-Nicene Fathers, 1, 6. Pp. 245-59. Rpt. Grand Rapids: Eerdmans, 1974.

Bertrand, G. M. *Saint Joseph dans les écrits des Pères de saint Justin à saint Pierre Chrysologue.* Theologia Montis Regii 45 = *Cahiers de Joséphologie* 14, 1. Montréal: Centre de recherche et de documentation, 1966.

Bover, Joseph M. "De S. Joseph S. Ephremi Syri Testimonia." *Ephemerides theologicae Lovanienses* 5 (1928): 221-24.

Brundage, James A. *Law, Sex, and Christian Society in Medieval Europe.* Chicago: University of Chicago Press, 1987.

Clark, Elizabeth A. "'Adam's Only Companion': Augustine and the Early Christian Debate on Marriage." *Recherches Augustiniennes* 21 (1986): 139-62.

Corbett, P. G. *The Roman Law of Marriage.* Oxford: Clarendon Press, 1930.

Doherty, Edward C. "Saint Augustine's Theology of Saint Joseph." *Tagastan* 20 (1958): 16-23.

Ehrhart, Arnold. "Nuptiae." RE 17, 2 (1937): 1478-89.

Filas, Francis L. *Joseph: The Man Closest to Jesus. The Complete Life, Theology and Devotional History of St. Joseph.* Boston: St. Paul Editions, 1962.

_____. *The Man Nearest to Christ: Nature and Historical Development of the Devotion to St. Joseph.* Milwaukee: Bruce, 1944.

_____. *St. Joseph after Vatican II: Conciliar Implications Regarding St. Joseph and His Inclusion in the Roman Canon.* Staten Island: Alba House, 1969.

Holzmeister, Urbanus. *De sancto Ioseph quaestiones biblicae.* Scripta Pontificii Instituti Biblici. Rome: Pontificium Institutum Biblicum, 1945.

Kübler. "Tabulae nuptiales." RE 2d series, 4, 2 (1932): 1949-55.

Kunkel. "Matrimonium." RE 14, 2 (1930): 2259-86.

Llamera, Boniface. *Saint Joseph.* Trans. Mary Elizabeth. St. Louis: Herder, 1962. (English translation of the following, without the work by Isidoro de Isolano, which the original includes.)

Llamera, Bonifacio. *Teología de San José, y edición bilingüe, versión e introducción . . . de la Suma de los dones de San José por Fr. Isidoro de Isolano.* Biblioteca de autores cristianos, 108. Madrid: Editorial Católica, 1953.

Noonan, John T. "Marital Affection in the Canonists." *Studia Gratiana* 12 (1967): 482-98.

Rasi, Piero. *Consensus facit nuptias*. Milan: A. Giuffrè, 1946.

Rondet, Henri. *Saint Joseph: Textes anciens avec une introduction*. Paris: Lethielleux, 1953.

Seitz, Joseph. *Die Verehrung des hl. Joseph in ihrer geschichtlichen Entwicklung bis zum Konzil von Trient dargestellt*. Freiburg: Herder, 1908.

Toschi, Larry M. *Joseph in the New Testament: With Redemptoris Custos, the Apostolic Exhortation of Pope John Paul II on Saint Joseph*. Santa Cruz: Guardian of the Redeemer Books, 1993.

Trottier, Aimé. *Essai de bibliographie sur saint Joseph*. 4th ed. 1955; Montreal: St. Joseph's Oratory, 1968.